*Awakening Your Soul
to the
Presence of God*

Kilian J. Healy, O. Carm.

Awakening
Your Soul
to the
Presence of God

How to Walk with Him Daily and
Dwell in Friendship with Him Forever

SOPHIA INSTITUTE PRESS®
Manchester, New Hampshire

Awakening Your Soul to the Presence of God: How to Walk with Him Daily and Dwell in Friendship with Him Forever was originally published in 1948 by the Declan X. McMullen Company, New York, under the title *Walking with God*. This 1999 edition by Sophia Institute Press contains minor editorial revisions to the original text.

Printed in the United States of America.

Cover design by Carolyn McKinney.

On the cover: "Sunset" (130618646)
© Vira Mylyan-Monastyrska / Shutterstock.com

Nihil obstat: The Very Rev. Matthew O'Neill, O. Carm.,
Provincial and *Censor Librorum*
Imprimatur: Samuel Cardinal Stritch,
Archbishop of Chicago, May 16, 1948

Sophia Institute Press
Box 5284, Manchester, NH 03108
1-800-888-9344

www.SophiaInstitute.com
Sophia Institute Press® is a registered trademark of Sophia Institute.

Library of Congress Cataloging-in-Publication Data
Healy, Kilian, 1912–
    Awakening your soul to the presence of God : how to walk with him daily and dwell in friendship with him forever / Kilian J. Healy.
      p.   cm.
    Rev. ed. of: Walking with God. c1948.
    Includes bibliographical references.
    ISBN 0-918477-42-5 (pbk. : alk. paper)
    1. Spiritual life — Catholic authors. I. Healy, Kilian, 1912– Walking with God. II. Title.
BX2350.2.H368   1999
248.4'82 — dc21   99-37816 CIP

To my mother and father

"Millions may hurry along the streets of great cities absorbed in their business or pleasure or sorrows, with never a thought of God. Yet the only true God is no less real. It is He who sustains them in their existence. Men and women must be brought to consciousness of the fact of God's existence, of their utter dependence on His power and love and mercy, and of their moral obligation to shape their daily lives according to His most holy will."

— *Pope Pius XII*

Editor's note: Except where otherwise noted, the biblical quotations in the following pages are based on the Douay-Rheims edition of the Old and New Testaments. Where applicable, quotations have been cross-referenced with the differing names and numeration in the Revised Standard Version, using the following symbol: (RSV =).

Contents

*Awakening Your Soul
to the
Presence of God*

Part One

Friendship with God

Chapter One

God desires your love

Some time ago, while on a train from Washington to New York, I became engaged in conversation with a young man. He was a graduate of a Catholic college, proud of the fact, and quite determined that the Faith was to be his guiding star through life.

A friend had recently given him a copy of the autobiography of St. Thérèse of Lisieux.[1] What surprised him most, he said, was the ease with which this young nun talked of her intimate friendship with God. Oh, he had learned in school that we are in this world to love God, but he had never known that this love could be an intimate, personal friendship. In his prayers, he was always most formal with God. He had always believed that he was loving God in the only way expected of him when he tried to observe the Ten Commandments and the precepts of the Church.

[1] St. Thérèse of Lisieux (1873-1897), Carmelite nun.

His relation to God had been one of duty and honor, like that of a soldier to his country. He found it quite natural to praise God. He enjoyed singing "Holy God, we praise Thy name," and one of his regular prayers was "Glory be to the Father, and to the Son, and to the Holy Spirit."

But he had never been taught to love God as a child loves his father. After all, God is a spirit, and it is not easy to think of Him as a Father. Prayers based on filial relationship seemed exaggerated. He had never realized that it is possible to *fall in love with God* — to think of Him continually, to try to please Him in all one's actions, as one thinks of and tries to please a person he loves. It had even seemed to him that intimate conversations with God were either expressions of pure sentimentality or pleasures to be enjoyed only in the next world.

I explained that falling in love with God is no mystery to those who are schooled in the saints or who are acquainted with some of the more ardent souls in religious life. It is the ideal of priests, brothers, nuns, and many devout laypeople. To say that falling in love with God is impossible is to deny an obvious fact: countless souls have done precisely that.

I ventured to say that perhaps he had never analyzed the full meaning of love. But I learned that he, like most young people, prided himself on knowing something about it. He believed in love, he told me — human love that occupies the whole mind and heart of the lover; love that becomes so much a part of a man that his thoughts turn continually to his beloved; love that tugs at the heartstrings and makes itself felt whenever the mind has a moment to itself.

When I smiled skeptically to show that I was not at all sure he knew what true love was, he quickly added that he was not considering only the emotional kind of love. He knew what true love is. It lasts forever, he said, even after the beauty and freshness of youth have vanished. You can see it in the eyes of the mother who spends sleepless nights watching over her sick child. You can see it in a husband who for years has devoted himself with amazing kindness and patience to an invalid wife. It is written on the haggard face of a young soldier as he drags his wounded comrade back from the front lines.

He had the right idea. He was not confusing love with emotionalism or sentimentality. Love *can* express itself through the emotions; it may manifest itself in the happiness and joy of a newly wedded couple or in the sadness that shrouds a family that has just lost its mother. It is clearly found in the life of Jesus. When He was told that Lazarus was dead, Jesus wept. And the people, seeing this, said, "Behold how He loved him."[2] True love can break forth and express itself in deep emotion, but it can also be externally cold — as unemotional as paying the income tax or washing dishes.

Love calls for self-giving

What, then, does loving someone really mean? It means that a person wants good to come to another; it is to *will* that good may come to him. True love is reasonable; it is not blind. It springs from the recognition of good that is grasped by the intellect and presented to the will as desirable. True love is also effective, demanding action from the lover, who feels driven to do something for the beloved.

Everyone, young or old, strong or weak, can love. But in this world, love is bound up with giving; it entails sacrifice. The highest kind of love means self-offering. Jesus

[2] John 11:36.

told us this: "Greater love than this no man hath, that a man lay down his life for his friends."[3]

It is easy to see that this is true of human love, but it is also true of love for God. What great love for Christ burned in the heart of St. Peter as he was crucified with his head in the dirt of the earth! Who can doubt the love of Paul for Jesus, as Paul was led outside the walls of Rome to be beheaded! And in our own day, who can help but marvel at the deep love of God that grew stronger day by day in the soul of St. Thérèse, the Little Flower, whose dying words were "My God, I love Thee!"

Some people may not be convinced by these examples. They may argue that they are isolated cases, coming shortly after conversion or accompanied by special help from God. And anyway, they may say, spur-of-the-moment heroism is not uncommon. But what of tender, intimate love of God spread over a whole lifetime? The fact that even busy laypeople can fall deeply in love with God — that is the mystery.

In human love, the lover always seeks his beloved. Separation is something very painful; presence, possession, is

---

[3] John 15:13.

an indescribable joy. Lovers talk to one another, even if they do not say much. Words are not weighed and studied with them; even the most insignificant words have a special meaning and are understood. A glance, an embrace, a sigh, a loving phrase — this is the language of lovers. It is *true* love, deeply felt and capable of raising the lover to the heights of heroism. It does not last for only a day or a week; it can endure for a lifetime — a lifetime of joy, or even of sorrow. It expresses itself in fidelity and wholehearted service.

Is such love possible between God and man? How can man be always with God, possessing Him, as the lover must? How can man carry on a loving conversation with God? Is this not merely wishful thinking?

Chapter Two

God calls you
to intimate friendship
with Him

It is quite possible to come to a profound love of God, but it will not be something that comes to us like a flash of lightning. Ordinarily, it will grow with time. For it is a love of friendship — wishing good to another. It grows in proportion as love for self decreases. Self-love decreases only after a difficult battle, but it is a battle that each and every one of us must fight. We have no alternative, for Christ has said, "Thou shalt love the Lord thy God with thy whole heart, and with thy whole soul."[4] Since God does not command the impossible, we can fall *out of* love with ourselves and *in* love with God. It is never too late to start.

This wholehearted love for God differs in many ways from love that creatures have for one another. First of all, our love of God can never end in disillusionment or tragedy. Human love can, and often does, as, for example,

[4] Mark 12:30.

when Antony was deceived by Cleopatra. Again, human love can end in tragedy when there is no return of love for love. Such was the sad case of Ophelia, who lost her mind when she was rejected. But there is no danger of Shakespearean tragedy when we love God. God is never unfaithful. He has never disappointed, and never will disappoint, the lover. He is our only true friend.

☞

God calls you to share in His life

Second, this friendship between God and man is a supernatural friendship that begins at the moment of Baptism, when we become the adopted children of God. Here, as in all friendships, there is a communication of gifts. On His part, God lifts us up above our human nature to share in His intimate life, to become a member of the family, a friend — somewhat after the manner of a slave who has been invited to sit at the table of his king, to become a member of the royal family and enjoy all its privileges of wealth and prestige.

When we come to the use of reason, this friendship develops into a conscious love of mutual well-wishing between God and our soul. Adopted into the family of God, we begin to know Him more intimately, not only

as our Creator, but as Father, Son, and Holy Spirit.
Sharing this knowledge, which belongs by right only
to the three divine Persons, we begin to love God as He
is in Himself. The pagans did not know of the three Persons in God. They asked how God could be happy alone.
"What does He think of, and whom does He love?" they
wondered. But we, by our Faith and our Christian vocation, know what God thinks and whom He loves.

We see Him as a loving Father, who sent His beloved
Son into the world to redeem us, that is, to restore us to
the friendship with Him that was lost by the sin of Adam.
We see Him confirming this friendship, sealing it by the
power of the Holy Spirit, whom He sends to dwell within
us. Hence, our friendship with God is one in which we
share the intimate secrets of the divine Persons and the
very life of God. We begin to share in the life of God, as
branches share the life of the vine, and as the body shares
the life of the soul.

It is true that, in this world, our sharing in the life
of God will always remain imperfect. But in Heaven,
this friendship will come to full bloom; the veil shall be
taken from our eyes, and we shall see God face-to-face
and embrace Him with an everlasting love.

Finally, of ourselves, we are not worthy to love God with the love of friendship. And, even so, it is impossible to have true love for God over a long period of time without special help from God, help that illumines our mind and inspires our will. But God never denies this help. Why, then, should it be impossible to think of God, to recognize Him as a loving Father, to call upon Him, to speak to Him personally, and to become so friendly with Him that life would lose its meaning, its happiness, if He were not there?

What more could God have done to invite us to be His friends? Did He not send His only-begotten Son into the world to become man, so that we might find it easier to know and to love Him? Did not Jesus say on the eve of His passion: "No longer do I call you servants . . . but I have called you friends"?[5] Was He not revealing to the Apostles and to the future members of the Church their vocation to intimacy with Him, the Son of God?

On our part, we have nothing to give God that will change Him or make Him richer. We do not enter this friendship for what we can get from it, but for what we

[5] John 15:15 (Revised Standard Version).

can put into it. It is not a selfish friendship, but a real friendship based on mutual communication of gifts. We must give God the best we have. We have only our thoughts to communicate to Him, only the love of our hearts to give Him, and only our poor actions, which we hope will praise Him and express our most profound thanks. Although these things are poor, if we give them, we give our all. And is he not a real friend who offers his life and work to the praise and glory of God?

God wants you to love Him for Himself

We must be careful, however, not to identify emotional consolation with the love we give God, just as we do not identify human love with the joyful emotions. We can love God without being sentimental. The emotions may play their part; God may send sensible sweetness, which is not to be despised — but such consolation is not necessary. It may happen that an intimate friend of God finds himself without any consolation, as was often the case with St. Thérèse of Lisieux. She says, "He [God] allowed my own soul to be plunged in thickest gloom, and the thought of Heaven, so sweet from my earliest years, to become for me a subject of torture. Nor did the trial last merely for days or weeks; months have passed in this agony, and I still await relief. I wish I could explain what I feel, but it is beyond my power. One must have passed through the tunnel to understand how black is its darkness."[6]

Not infrequently, a friend of God may find himself depressed, overcome with worry, or fearful that God is displeased and has withdrawn His grace. In this sense, we can understand the plaintive cry of the lover: "I adjure you, O daughters of Jerusalem, if you find my beloved, that you tell him that I languish with love."[7]

No matter what the emotions may be, our friendship with God remains steadfast. We are always conscious by faith that God returns our love. It is this faith that moves us to talk to God in joy or sorrow. As this friendship with God grows, we begin to put on the mind of God — to think as He thinks, to judge all things according to their eternal value and not according to their temporary usefulness. We begin to love God for Himself, and not because He is good to us. We learn to will all things that

[6] Thomas N. Taylor, trans., *A Little White Flower* (Chicago: Carmelite Press, n.d.), 185.
[7] Cant. 5:8 (RSV = Song of Sol. 5:8).

He wills, to seek His will and not our own. This is real friendship with God, for it ends in the union of our mind and will with His. Between God and us, there is one mind, one desire, one affection.

While we are the true friends of God and talk to Him about our joys and needs, we never forget that we are also His creatures, enriched by Him, yet infinitely beneath Him. We never lose sight of the service we owe to God in the fulfillment of His commandments. This service is no longer one of fear, nor a service founded on obedience only, but one that flows from love.

This vocation to be an intimate friend of God is not beyond our reach. It is obligatory, to a degree, and God would not hold something out to us, beckon us to receive it, and then gradually withdraw it.

How are we to acquire it? Is there a short, practical way within our power by which we can come to a deep, tender love of God?

Chapter Three

Loving recollection of God's presence leads to friendship with Him

"We learn to love by loving." As a general principle, that is quite self-evident. But it can be applied in many different ways. Some people shy away from following any special road to the love of God that appears systematized or scientific. They argue that, since we learn to love by loving, the best way to come to a deep, tender love of God is by beginning to love Him and forgetting about any special rules.

But it is not enough to be told to start loving God and, after that, all will go well. Usually, all does not go well. Many people have desired divine friendship, only to find that, after months and years of fidelity to prayer and the commandments, they are still strangers to God. They have been driving in the night without any light to guide them. They know where they want to go, but there seems to be no one to direct them. For them, we propose a way of love that leads quickly and directly to divine intimacy. It is called the exercise of the presence of God.

Awakening Your Soul to the Presence of God

This exercise is not a new method of prayer. It is not
even, properly speaking, a method, because it does not
bind us to follow a set pattern of rules. It simplifies prayer
without making it less effective. As we shall see, this exercise, when brought to perfection, makes us continually
aware of God and enables us to converse continually
with Him. And, like all conversations of lovers, it is not
made up of many words, but of profound silent desires
and sighs that become part of our very being, almost as
regular and natural as our breathing.

Of course, it is not possible for even the most perfect
person to be conscious of God's presence for twenty-four
hours a day. But it is quite possible to think of God and
be actively conscious of Him frequently throughout the
day, just as a loving mother, although busy with house-
work, can be continually preoccupied in mind and heart
with her sick child.

The exercise of the presence of God is for all men at
all times; indeed, we find it practiced wherever men live
close to God. The early Fathers of the Church used it, and
spiritual writers throughout the ages have never ceased
to champion it. It is for the beginner in prayer as well as
the saint, for the unlearned as well as the learned, for the

layman as well as the religious and priest. It admits of so many degrees that there is no state in the spiritual life of man wherein it cannot be used. It is, therefore, for you.

Before we go further, let us analyze what we mean by the "presence of God." Strictly speaking, it is any act of the memory or of the intellect by which we believe or recall that God is present. We can, for example, imagine God before us, or even in us. We can (although this is contrary to reality) picture Him as a venerable old man with a white beard, or we can even imagine Him pervading the atmosphere as air does — as an ethereal being. Better yet, we can imagine the Son of God made man, standing before us in all His glorious majesty, just as He stood before Mary Magdalene after rising glorious from death on that first Easter Sunday.

If we find it difficult to form an image of Christ, then, as St. Teresa of Avila[8] did, we can keep a picture of Him to look at from time to time. Or we can even think of Christ as present without forming any clear image; that is, we can make a simple act of faith that He is within us: "O God, I believe that Thou art within me."

[8] St. Teresa of Avila (1515-1582), Carmelite nun and mystic.

⁀

God is present to every creature

This act of faith is based upon fact. God is really present to us, and in many ways. For the moment, let it suffice to say that God is present to every creature in at least three ways: by His knowledge, His essence, and His power.

By His knowledge: God not only knows our every thought, desire, and action, but He knew us before we ever existed. He knows our eternal destiny. He is more conscious of us than we are of ourselves. "And there is no creature hidden from His sight, but all things are naked and open to the eyes of Him to whom we have to give account."[9]

By His essence: God not only knows us, but He created us and sustains us in existence every moment of our lives. God is wholly and entirely present to all things by His essence, because, wherever He acts, His whole being is there; there is no separation of His action from His essence.

By His power: We are not only from God, but we still belong to God. He not only holds us, as it were, by the hand, but He sustains us in existence. We and all

---

[9] Cf. Heb. 4:13.

creatures are controlled by His all-embracing power; were He for one moment to withdraw His sustaining power, we would cease to exist.

So, God is very close to us. In fact, He is within us. He is more intimate to us than our own thoughts, although remaining distinct from us. Hence, if we really want to be human, we shall never try to escape from God (which in any case is impossible), for, when we deliberately try to live without God, we cease to act as human beings. We should, therefore, try not only to think of Him, but to think *with* Him, conscious of His ever-abiding presence and of our absolute dependence. We should consider it a pleasure to walk along the road of life hand in hand with God.

⊂

Love arises from awareness of God's presence

It would be a mistake to think that recollection of God and belief in His presence are sufficient to make us His friend. For it is possible to think of God and hate Him. It is possible to study about God, learn all about His divine nature, believe all the divine truths, yet never raise our hearts to love Him. Our relationship with God could be like that of people who live in the same apartment house and remain total strangers. They know each other, talk about each other, but never speak to each other.

Therefore, if the practice of living in God's presence is to unite us to Him in love, it must do more than teach us to think of Him. It must teach us to be attracted to Him, to love and speak intimately with Him, as a child with his father. In other words, it must include acts of the will, affections, by which we long for God and speak to Him in short, affectionate prayers.

The exercise of the presence of God leads us to intimate love of God, and indirectly leads us away from sin and worldliness. The more we grow in this practice, the less power the pleasures of the world have over us. When we have learned to live in God's presence, things that once delighted us will lose their attraction. Their appeal will be like that of childhood toys to adults. Carried on by enthusiasm like that of Christ with His face set toward Jerusalem and Calvary, outstripping His Apostles on the road,[10] the soul that has learned to live in God's presence looks continually toward God, unperturbed by the allurements of the passing pleasures of life.

[10] Cf. Mark 10:32.

You must desire to live in God's presence

Many people remain strangers to God because they love unwisely the pleasures of the flesh and the world. They would love God, but they want the inordinate love of creatures, too. Having known the pleasures of this life, they find it almost impossible to give them up. They fear, and how foolishly, that nothing can take the place of human loves, money, sports, and carnal pleasures. But, if they were to set out to love God, to live in His presence, they would find their love of creatures gradually diminishing. To one who sees God, all created things are small. Having loved a greater good, it is easy to forget the lesser: "If a man should give all the substance of his house for love, he shall despise it as nothing."[11]

In this exercise, as in all progress in prayer, it is most important to persevere. We must have the desire to want to live in the presence of God. We must pray for this desire. We must not be satisfied only to be in the state of grace. We must continually bestir ourselves to realize that it is possible to come to deep love of God. We must

[11] Cant. 8:7 (RSV = Song of Sol. 8:7).

renew this desire again and again, because, once we lose sight of God, we shall turn to fill our minds with worldly things that please only the senses.

There is, then, a short, direct way to intimacy with God. It is short, but not easy. We call it the exercise of the presence of God. It contains two actions: one of the intellect, the other of the will. In the first action, we think of God; in the second, we desire to be with Him and to speak to Him. The phrase "presence of God," therefore, is not restricted to the acts of the memory or intellect alone, but is extended to include also the acts of the will, affections and aspirations. It is in this wider sense that we shall speak of the exercise of the presence of God. As we grow in this exercise, we shall grow in closer union with God, so that we will not only begin to think *of* Him, but *with* Him, and to love what He loves.

It is one thing to know what the exercise of the presence of God is and another to find ways to put it into action. To help put it into action, we will now present five practical ways of living with God. Finally, we will show how these different ways can be woven into the pattern of everyday life, so that we no longer walk alone, but with God.

Part Two

*How to experience
God's presence*

Chapter Four

See God in creation

The first way of learning to live with God so as to love Him dearly is to elevate the mind to Him through the visible things around us. Wherever we go, God is there: "If I ascend into Heaven, Thou art there. If I descend into hell, Thou art present. If I take my wings early in the morning, and dwell in the uttermost parts of the sea, even there also shall Thy hand lead me, and Thy right hand shall hold me."[12]

Whatever we look at, God is within it. Look at the sun. It brings light and warmth into our life. It reflects the goodness of God, who has created it. Gaze at the moon and the stars. They are the lanterns placed by God in the heavens to guide the weary traveler. Bless God who has made them, for the heavens and earth are full of His glory: "Look upon the rainbow, and bless Him that made it: it is very beautiful in its brightness. It encompasseth the

[12] Ps. 138:8-10 (RSV = Ps. 139:8-10).

heaven about with the circle of its glory; the hands of the Most High have displayed it."[13]

So, the beauty of nature reflects the beauty of God. For those who will not close their eyes, and who harden not their hearts, beautiful things are seen as the finger-prints of God. "A whirlwind and clouds are the dust of His feet."[14] All things are His messengers, making known His goodness, His justice, and His power.

⌒

Even commonplace things reflect God

Even the more commonplace things lead man to God. After eating a well-prepared dinner, most people sing the praises of the cook — and that is as it should be. But why not also praise God? He is the great Provider: from His hands all good things come, the food as well as the cook.

There is nothing more commonplace than sickness and death. They, too, can lead us to God. Some people face sickness and death with a resigned, hopeless attitude. It must come, they say, and there is nothing to do about it. Others become angry with God because He permits

[13] Ecclus. 43:12-13 (RSV = Sir. 43:11-12).
[14] Nah. 1:3.

evil in their lives. A third class recognizes sickness and death as a warning from God, that here we have no lasting city.[15] These people see the vanity of great wealth and earthly glory, which they cannot take with them. For this group, sickness and death become graces that lead them to think of God, to turn to Him, and to love Him above all the things of this world.

How foolish it is, then, to seek God first in the strange and spectacular. Rather, He is to be found in common, ordinary things. When God became man, He chose for His mother a quiet, unknown woman. His birthplace was not a palace, but a cave. During His life, He walked and talked with ordinary people. He chose fishermen as His companions. He did not dine with Herod, but in the homes of common people. He was crucified between two common thieves. He can be found where the unspiritual least expect to find Him — in common things.

Christ, always the great teacher, taught his Apostles to see and reflect on the attributes of God mirrored in commonplace things. "See how the lilies of the field grow; they neither toil nor spin, yet I say to you that not

---

[15] Cf. Heb. 13:14.

even Solomon in all his glory was arrayed like one of these. But if God so clothes the grass of the field, which today is alive and tomorrow is thrown into the oven, how much more you, O you of little faith!"[16]

In His parables, the Savior gave earthly things heavenly meanings: the kingdom of God is like a net cast into the sea, or a mustard seed, or a pearl.[17] And St. Paul brought out the same idea, holding the pagans who did not believe in God inexcusable, "seeing that what may be known about God is manifest to them. For God has manifested it to them. For since the creation of the world, His invisible attributes are clearly seen — His everlasting power also and divinity — being understood through the things that are made."[18]

St. Thérèse of Lisieux admired the beauty of God and His glory as it was reflected in flowers. And even as a child, she was carried away by the power of God which she found mirrored in the sea. "I was between six and seven when I saw the sea for the first time. I could not turn away my eyes: its majesty, the roaring of the waves,

[16] Matt. 6:28-30 (Revised Standard Version).
[17] Cf. Matt. 13:47, 31, 46.
[18] Rom. 1:19-20.

the whole vast spectacle impressed me deeply and spoke to my soul of God's power and greatness."[19]

And St. Ignatius counseled, with regard to the Jesuit students, that they should exercise themselves "in finding God our Lord in all things, in conversation, in walking, seeing, tasting, hearing, thinking, and, in fact, in all kinds of activity, for of a truth the majesty of God is in all things."[20] Is it not clear that even the most ordinary things in our daily lives can lift us up to God, who made them?

Needless to say, this exercise is not to be exaggerated. We would become nervous and distracted if we continually searched outside of ourselves for things and events that would remind us of God's presence. We would soon acquire a strong dislike for this exercise. It is sufficient to raise our mind to God when the occasion offers itself. At times, the Holy Spirit will give us these thoughts, and it is then that we should willingly accept them, and never shut them out through our own fault. Progress will be slow at first, because our mind is not yet turned to God,

[19] A Little White Flower, 41.
[20] Johannes Lindworsky, S.J., The Psychology of Asceticism (London: H. W. Edwards, 1936), 68; St. Ignatius of Loyola (c. 1491-1556), founder of the Society of Jesus.

but the more we turn toward Him, the more natural this act will become. Eventually, we will see the hand of God in all things, not only in the rhapsodic beauty of a spring day, but in common events — even in the evils of society and in everyday life.

⌒

Daily circumstances can remind you of God

A young college student once told me how he learned to think of God and pray to Him frequently. Every school day, he had to walk a mile and a half to class. Along the way, through the back streets of the city, over hills and down alleys, he met many people hurrying to work or to school. He would pray for the poorly clad or sickly, at the same time thanking God for his own better condition and health. When he passed churches, he thought of Jesus in the Blessed Sacrament. If there was time, he would make a visit; otherwise, he would think of Jesus as he passed by. He made short acts of adoration, thanksgiving, and petition.

It gave him special delight to say a prayer for small children playing near their homes or on their way to school. He sought God's protection upon salesmen opening up their stores and upon businessmen hurrying to work. He

prayed for non-Catholics and for their conversion as
he passed their churches. He prayed for his teachers, his
classmates, and for success in school. And, because he
was a very normal young man, and quite attached to a
young lady, his thoughts were often of her; he prayed that
God would always bless her and that Mary would always
protect her.

Naturally, he had many distractions on the way to
school. Sometimes, companions would join him; sometimes, he would be lost in thought over a school problem
or a football game. But he would always come back to
think of God. His thoughts were passing; his prayers were
short — most of them only a few words. On some days he
prayed more than on others, but every day found him seeing God in the world around him.

Later, before he finished school, he was drafted into
the army. Long nights of sentry duty found him alone
with his thoughts. Here, the good habit of thinking of
God brought comfort and peace to his heart. He prayed
to God throughout the long hours of the night, as he
walked along beneath the stars.

A train engineer once said that, during his many years
of service, he never had an accident. In fact, his whole

life was a blessed one. He attributed this blessing of
God to an unwavering trust in His Providence. On his
nightly run across the country, he passed many Catholic
churches. In time he knew them all, and in each one he
saluted his eucharistic King. As his train rushed on in the
night, he thought of Jesus, who watched over each parish
and town from the tabernacle. In many of the churches,
he could see the light of the sanctuary lamp reflected on
the stained-glass windows, and he would raise his heart
in prayer: "O Jesus in the Blessed Sacrament, all praise to
Thee. Watch over Thy people, and watch over me and
those whom Thou hast placed in my care."

The young college student and the engineer were not
far advanced in prayer. There was great room for progress.
But they had begun well; with time, their love of God
would grow.

What they learned to do, we also can do. Remember
always that, wherever we go, God is there. Whatever we
look at, God is within it. "For He is not far away from
each one of us; in Him we live and move and have our
being."[21]

---

[21] Acts 17:27-28 (Revised Standard Version).

Chapter Five

Listen to God
speaking to you

It is one thing to search for God and another to listen to Him once we have found Him. Many people never listen to God because they are not aware that He speaks to them. Yet, God does speak. One way to live in His presence is to acquire the habit of recognizing His voice when He speaks. If we do not know that God wishes to communicate with us, or the ways He has chosen, then our passage through life will be devoid of the most perfect of guides.

When does God speak to us? He speaks at all times, especially in prayer. Prayer is a conversation with God. But it is not a monologue. When we pray, then, we should also listen, because a good conversationalist is also a good listener. We do not pray well when we recite ready-made formulas quickly and distractedly. We act as if God has only to listen to us, and that we have no need to listen to the thoughts and desires that He wishes to communicate to us. He has promised, "If thou wilt hear the voice of the Lord thy God, and do what is right before Him, and obey

His commandments, and keep all His precepts, none of the evils that I laid upon Egypt will I bring upon thee."[22]

Unfortunately, many of us have never trained ourselves to listen to His voice. But, if we are to know God's will, we must listen to Him and obey Him when we recognize His commandments.

But how does God speak to us? God is a pure spirit. Unlike man, He has no voice. If He wishes to speak to us, He must use some means outside of Himself, adapted to our nature, by which He can communicate ideas. He may use things we can see and hear in order to stir our imagination, or He may enter directly into our thoughts. He may do this miraculously, but ordinarily He communicates with us according to the established laws of nature.

☞

God speaks through creation

One very simple way that God speaks to us is through the sacramental universe. Through the world of beauty, God tells us about Himself: "All men who were ignorant of God were foolish by nature; and they were unable, from the good things that are seen, to know Him who

[22] Exod. 15:26.

exists, nor did they recognize the Craftsman while paying heed to His works. If, through delight in the beauty of these things, men assumed them to be gods, let them know how much better than these is their Lord, for the Author of beauty created them."[23]

All creation is the voice of the Lord. Those who do not recognize His power, love, mercy, and justice, reflected in these creatures He has made, are not to be pardoned. "For if they had the power to know so much that they could investigate the world, how did they fail to find sooner the Lord of these things?"[24]

God speaks through direct revelation

But the wise God has chosen a more direct and startling way to speak to man. He spoke to Moses from a burning bush: "And when the Lord saw that he went forward to see, He called to him out of the midst of the bush, and said, 'Moses, Moses.' And he answered, 'Here I am.' . . . And He said, 'I am the God of thy father, the God of Abraham, the God of Isaac, and the God of Jacob.' "[25]

[23] Cf. Wisd. 13:1, 3 (Revised Standard Version).
[24] Wisd. 13:9 (Revised Standard Version).
[25] Exod. 3:4, 6.

Moses was only one of many chosen souls. God selected prophets from among the Jews, and He enlightened their minds so that they might carry His message to the people. Isaiah, Micah, Ezekiel, and a host of other prophets brought words of comfort and of warning to the chosen race.

Jeremiah, the great prophet, tells us how God spoke to him: "And the Lord put forth His hand and touched my mouth; and the Lord said to me: Behold I have given my words in thy mouth."[26]

The word God spoke to the prophets has been recorded in writing. God also inspired other men, who were not prophets, to write down the message He wished to give the world. All these writings, which were given under the inspiration of the Holy Spirit, can be found in Sacred Scripture.

Some of them record the words that God Himself spoke through His only-begotten Son, Jesus Christ. St. Paul tells us this: "God, who at sundry times and in diverse manners spoke in times past to the fathers by the prophets, last of all in these days has spoken to us by His

[26] Jer. 1:9.

Son, whom He appointed heir of all things, by whom also
He made the world."[27]

⌒

God speaks through His Church

When the Son of God departed from this world, He
gave us the Church, His Mystical Body, as the instrument
to guide us to perfection. If we listen to the Church and
obey the Church, we obey God Himself. The Liturgy of
the Church emphasizes for us much that is contained in
Sacred Scripture. The Sacrifice of the Mass, the heart of
the Church's Liturgy, is the principal example of this; the
readings and the Gospel of the Mass, as well as the essen-
tial words of consecration, are taken from the Word of
God. Is it any wonder that the Liturgy is often called the
revelation of God to man?

⌒

God speaks to you personally

Does God, then, speak to man? How can we ever
doubt it? How foolish it is to read all types of books and
neglect the word of God! The Scriptures were not meant
only for particular groups of people; they were meant for

[27] Heb. 1:1-2.

all men at all times. God is eternal; His words are eternal. Although He speaks to all men, He speaks to us personally.

This does not mean that every person should take the Bible and interpret it according to his own fancy. No, the Church alone is the divinely appointed authority to guide us in the correct interpretation of the Bible. The Church encourages us to read it, because she knows that the word of God can enter into our minds and that God, in His own mysterious way, can teach the true way of life, the way of love and intimate union with Him.

It is quite true, then, to say that God speaks to each one of us personally when we read, "Come to me, all you who labor and are burdened, and I will refresh you."[28] "If any man will come after me, let him deny himself, and take up his cross, and follow me."[29] "This is my commandment, that you love one another as I have loved you."[30]

St. Ignatius of Loyola felt that God was speaking directly to him, when, on his sick bed, he read the words:

[28] Matt. 11:28.
[29] Matt. 16:24.
[30] John 15:12.

"For what shall it profit a man if he gain the whole world, and suffer the loss of his soul?"[31]

But, we ask, is this *prayer?* It is at least the beginning of prayer. We listen to these words of Christ; we ponder over them; they awaken thoughts and desires within us. We begin to believe, to hope, to love. Our will becomes inspired, and we break forth in ardent affections, calling on Christ to help us, begging forgiveness, expressing gratitude, performing little acts of adoration — and surely *this* is prayer.

We often read of visions, apparitions, and revelations in which God spoke to the saints. St. Paul on the road to Damascus is a classic example.[32] And we read in the life of St. Margaret Mary Alacoque[33] that, while she was engaged in prayer, Jesus often spoke to her of the devotion to His Sacred Heart.

Such conversations with God are not rare in the lives of the canonized. But must *we* in our conversation with

---

[31] Mark 8:36.

[32] Cf. Acts 9:3-7.

[33] St. Margaret Mary Alacoque (1647-1690), Visitation nun who was the chief founder of devotion to the Sacred Heart of Jesus.

God await the appearance of Jesus, of some heavenly voice or extraordinary apparition, some heavenly manifestation from God? Absolutely not. It is true that God does single out some chosen souls to whom He speaks directly and who actually experience the divine power working in them, but these are very few; it is not the way that God ordinarily uses. We should not even desire that God speak to us in this extraordinary manner. We should not expect it. Visions and revelations are not necessary for us to grow in deep love for God. We may fall deeply in love with Him and practice faithfully the presence of God, yet never receive any extraordinary manifestations from Him. These are special gifts, and God gives them to whom He wills, and when He wills.

☞

God speaks to your mind and to your heart

Nevertheless, God does speak to all of us without exception in a more direct way than we have yet mentioned. It is a hidden way, by which He enters directly into our thoughts and desires. Our most hidden secrets are not secrets to Him. He comes right into our mind. Our thoughts are not only our thoughts; our desires are not only our desires — they may also be God's thoughts and desires. We know we can do nothing without God. Even such ordinary things as eating, breathing, and walking cannot be done without the ordinary help that God gives us. But, in this instance, we are presupposing this natural help of God and are referring to a greater and more noble assistance from Him.

Does God help us in a special way to think good thoughts and to desire holy things? He most assuredly does. For we are living in a supernatural order and destined to a supernatural end, the Beatific Vision. To attain this end, God not only gives us the principle of supernatural life, sanctifying grace, but He also gives us actual graces that help us to perform supernatural actions and thus to grow in the grace of God. These actual graces are, especially, the holy thoughts and desires that God creates in us.

God does not have to use external words and signs to attract our attention and convey ideas to us. He enters our minds directly. He speaks secretly, noiselessly, as befits the Divinity. It is only by faith that we know He is working in us. For example, God once spoke in a special, hidden way to St. Peter, who then confessed Jesus to be the Son of God. "Blessed art thou, Simon Bar-Jona," said our Lord. "For flesh and blood hath not revealed this to thee, but my Father in Heaven."[34]

St. John tells us that we will know all things from the Holy Spirit: "But you have an anointing from the Holy One, and you know all things."[35] St. Paul says that God enters our very thoughts: "Not that we are sufficient to think anything of ourselves, as of ourselves, but our sufficiency is from God."[36]

God also enters our hearts and inspires us to holy desires. "And a certain woman named Lydia, a seller of purple, from the city of Thyatira, who worshiped God, was listening; and the Lord touched her heart to give heed to what was being said by Paul."[37]

Thus, the Scriptures and the Church tell us that God speaks to us in the silence of our minds and hearts. He speaks to all men, but all men do not hear Him.

God speaks to our mind and heart when we kneel to meditate or to adore Him in the Blessed Sacrament. He enters our mind when the passing things of time excite

[34] Matt. 16:17.
[35] Cf. 1 John 2:20.
[36] 2 Cor. 3:5.
[37] Acts 16:14 (Revised Standard Version).

our thoughts. It is He who gives us holy thoughts to con-
quer our temptations. It is He who stirs up within us the
desire to persevere against all adversaries.

Perhaps we have never realized that God is illuminat-
ing our intellect and inspiring our will. Yet He does just
that. That is why we are told not to do all the talking in
prayer. For, if we continually recite vocal prayers without
pausing now and then to think, we will stifle the thoughts
and desires that God wishes to excite in us.

St. Thérèse of Lisieux tells us how she listened to the
voice of God. "I know and have experienced that 'the
Kingdom of God is within us,' that our Master has no
need of books or teacher to instruct a soul. The Teacher
of teachers instructs without sound of words, and though
I have never heard Him speak, yet I know He is within
me, always guiding and inspiring me; and just when I
need them, lights, hitherto unseen, break in upon me.
As a rule, it is not during prayer that this happens, but
in the midst of my daily duties."[38]

But we are not only to listen; it would be folly to remain in a state of mental blankness, waiting for God to

[38] A *Little White Flower*, 173.

speak. No, prayer is a loving conversation, and, when the Holy Spirit moves us, it is time to begin our part of the colloquy.

One way, then, to practice the exercise of the presence of God is to listen to God, to be aware that He speaks to us, to be ever conscious that God can use all things to communicate with us.

You will learn gradually to live in God's presence

First, a warning: we cannot change overnight our way of living with God. But then, we do not learn to typewrite in one or two lessons, either. We must first accustom our fingers to one group of keys, then to another, until we have mastered them all. So, too, in learning to live continually with God and in learning to converse with Him, we must proceed gradually and in an orderly manner. Day by day we must progress, seeing the hand of God in all things, being aware that He speaks to us and manifests His will in the joys, sorrows, and circumstances of our daily life.

Chapter Six

Develop friendship with Jesus

One of the easiest ways to live in God's presence is to look upon Jesus, the divine Son of God. The Son of God became man so that man might become, in turn, the adopted son and friend of God. In becoming man, God has made it easier for us to understand His love for us. Witness His gentle appeal: "Learn of me, for I am meek and humble of heart."[39] "No longer do I call you servants . . . but I have called you friends."[40]

Such an appeal makes it much easier for us to approach Him than it was for the chosen people before Christ, who never saw God and knew Him only as the Divine Spirit. But we, through the humanity of Christ, find ready access to union with the Divinity. The man Jesus of Nazareth, who was born in Bethlehem, who walked along the dusty roads of Galilee, who talked to

[39] Matt. 11:29.
[40] John 15:15 (Revised Standard Version).

the woman at the well of Jacob,[41] who raised Lazarus from the dead,[42] and who finally died on the Cross, was truly the Son of God.

☙

Union with Christ means union with God

Since Jesus is one with God the Father, union with Jesus — even in this world — is the purpose of our life. He is the One whom we must love most deeply, so that we may reach the perfection of nature and find true happiness. To love Jesus of Nazareth with an intimate, personal love is to love God with an intimate, personal love, for Jesus is God.

Therefore, if we have Jesus in His sacred humanity ever before our eyes, if we look upon Him with love and try to live a life of personal friendship with Him, pleasing Him in all things, we will have already attained, to some degree, an intimate love of God.

Now we can understand why it is so helpful to meditate on the life of Jesus and why St. Teresa of Avila could suggest this method to her nuns: "The soul can picture

---

[41] John 4:6-26.
[42] john 11:43-44.

itself in the presence of Christ, and accustom itself to become enkindled with great love for His sacred humanity and to have Him ever with it and speak with Him, ask Him for the things it has need of, make complaints to Him of its trials, rejoice with Him in its joys, and yet never allow its joys to make it forgetful of Him. It has no need to think out set prayers but can use just such words as suit its desires and needs."[43]

We may represent our Lord in many different manners, depending on the disposition and the state of holiness we have attained. If we are just a beginner, we might find it advantageous to perform our daily work in the presence of Christ, imagining Him to be nearby, using some holy card or painting for our image of Him.

If we have learned to pray and to live a virtuous life, this simple imaginary presence will not satisfy us. We will want to read and reread the Gospels, make a study of Christ, and then try to walk in His footsteps — even to the Cross. Only the continual study of Christ can make us *conscious* of His presence and ensure our imitation of Him.

[43] E. Allison Peers, ed. and trans., *The Complete Works of St. Teresa of Jesus* (New York: Sheed and Ward, 1946), Vol. 1, 71.

⌒

Circumstances can help you think of Christ

Let us see how we might put this into practice. We
find that our work and efforts are not appreciated by
those whom we are trying to help. At such times, do
we think of Christ deserted by the Apostles, when the
soldiers came to seize Him?[44] His own believed Him a
failure.

Perhaps the monotony of everyday life begins to wear
us down, and there seems to be no hope of change. Do
we recall Christ, the model of patience, waiting thirty
years to reveal His mission to the world? Do we at least
pray to Him, feeling confident that He can help us?

Or, perhaps we are poor. Christ Himself often slept
by the seashore.

Or, we are snubbed, called a fool. Was not Christ
shunted from Pilate to Herod to Pilate again?[45] Should
our lot be better?

Or, we suffer terrible physical or mental pain. There
is no apparent reason why we should suffer. But the

[44] Cf. Matt. 26:56.
[45] Cf. Luke 23:7, 11.

innocent Christ wore a crown of thorns and was nailed to the Cross. Should we be better off than the Son of God? He was innocent. Are we innocent of every sin?

The liturgical year is beautifully arranged to make us conscious of the role Christ can play in our life. The Child in the crib can awaken within us an attraction to His life of poverty, obedience, and simplicity. When we look at Him in the crib, we see more than a helpless baby. We see the Lamb who came to take away the sins of the world. We see the Peacemaker between God and man. During Lent, and especially at Passiontide, the Church can teach us to carry the Cross and live the Passion in our daily life. And for those who would like to think of Christ and imagine Him as He really is in His glorified human body, the Church presents the Liturgy of Easter Sunday and the immediately succeeding weeks.

☞

You can attain continual communion with Christ

But, again, we must use daily effort in order to make any progress. Just as a child learning to walk must first learn to crawl, then to stand with support, then take a few steps alone, until gradually he can walk with steady step, so also the child who reaches out to God and desires to live in continual communion with Him must, as a general rule, first go through all the stages of spiritual walking.

Some people may think that this living in the presence of Jesus in His sacred humanity is impossible. But is it not true that mothers who love their children live continually in their presence? Why, then, should it be impossible for those who love Jesus to think of Him often and try to please Him?

Jesus has always held first place in the thoughts of holy Christian men and women. St. Paul, the Apostle of the Gentiles, after the apparition on the road to Damascus, lived continually in the presence of Jesus. He preached one gospel: Jesus crucified and our new life in Him. "For I decided to know nothing among you, except Jesus Christ, and Him crucified."[46]

The spirit of St. Paul is still alive in the Church. In our own day, this is well illustrated in the life of Fr. Titus Brandsma, O. Carm., who was at one time Rector of the Catholic University of Nijmegen, Holland, and an authority in the field of Carmelite mysticism. In 1942, the

[46] 1 Cor. 2:2 (Revised Standard Version).

Nazis sent Fr. Titus to the dreaded concentration camp
of Dachau, where he was isolated in an unused dog ken-
nel and forced to mimic the barking of a dog each time a
guard passed. After great torture and suffering, the aged
priest died on July 26, 1942. The Nazis sent his breviary
to his confreres in Holland, but they had failed to notice
that the priest had inserted between the lines of the breviary the story of his suffering. And there, too, he had
written his last song, a real prayer, a conversation with
Jesus. In the hour of his greatest affliction, he could converse intimately with our Lord, since, during his life, he
had learned to live in His presence:

> A new awareness of Thy love
> Encompasses my heart:
> Sweet Jesus, I in Thee and Thou
> In me shall never part.
>
> No grief shall fall my way, but I
> Shall see Thy grief-filled eyes;
> The lonely way that Thou once walked
> Has made me sorrow-wise.
>
> All trouble is a white-lit joy
> That lights my darkest day;

Thy love has turned to brightest light
This night-like way.

If I have Thee alone,
The hours will bless
With still, cold hands of love
My utter loneliness.

Stay with me, Jesus, only stay;
I shall not fear
If, reaching out my hand,
I feel Thee near.

Chapter Seven

Offer each day to God

Another way to live in the presence of God is to offer ourselves and all our actions to God the Father in union with Jesus crucified. This way of prayer is often called the morning offering. It is more than a prayer; it is really a way of life keeping us in constant touch with God in all our daily thoughts, desires, and actions. Through the morning offering, we walk no longer alone, but in the presence of Christ crucified, whose perfect surrender of His life to His Father we strive to imitate in all our actions.

Pope Pius XII, in his encyclical on the Mystical Body of Christ, recommended the daily offering of the Apostleship of Prayer to all the faithful:

O Jesus, through the Immaculate Heart of Mary,
I offer Thee my prayers, works, and sufferings of this day
in union with the Holy Sacrifice of the Mass throughout
the world, in reparation for my sins, and for the
intentions recommended by the Holy Father.

Awakening Your Soul to the Presence of God

Or you may use the short form, which gives the
substance of this prayer:

Jesus, through the Immaculate Heart of Mary,
I offer Thee this day all my thoughts, words,
actions, joys, and sufferings.

Many of us have practiced the morning offering since
early school days, but often it has not colored our lives.
Too many have been content to offer each day to God
and then go about their daily affairs without further
thought of what they have promised. For them, the
morning offering is an isolated prayer that does not lead
them to personal love of God and friendship with Him.
Unwittingly, they consider the morning offering a duty,
the right thing to do for one who professes belief in
Christ. Somehow, it does not occur to them that the
morning offering is an introduction to an intimate,
friendly life with God. They are quite satisfied to do
things *for* God on special occasions. They are not aware
that God is asking them to do *all* things *with* Him.

The morning offering extends its influence beyond
our waking thoughts. It implies giving ourselves, surren-
dering our wills in all things as Christ surrendered His

will in the Garden of Olives and on the Cross. The morning offering really means that we strive to live in the presence of Jesus and that we unite the offering of ourselves with His offering on the Cross. It means we live and work *with* Christ, offering ourselves to God the Father to carry out the work of salvation of souls begun on Calvary and destined to be completed in the Church and through the Church. This is truly our vocation, because at Baptism we have been made one with Christ. In the words of St. Leo the Great:[47] "Baptism has made us flesh of the Crucified One." We must, therefore, strive to live continually in the presence of Christ, that is, to be mentally and effectively aware of Him to whom we are most intimately bound by the ties of the Redemption.

Your offering must come from your heart

The most important thing to remember is that the morning offering should be renewed frequently during each day. It is this continual renewal of the morning offering that changes man's way of living and makes him Christlike.

---

[47] St. Leo I (d. 461), Pope from 440.

Of course, the mere recitation of the prayer, no matter how frequently, will not bring about the change. Reciting prayers can become mere lip service. The morning offering and its renewal will affect our way of living only if it comes from a soul that thinks of God and desires to do His will. If the offering comes from the heart, if there is a determination to perform all the actions of the day for the love of God, for His glory, and for the salvation of souls, then the offering will bear fruit.

The morning offering is a good way to start the day. But let us actually give our thoughts and actions to God. How insincere it is to make the offering and then to complain about the weather, lack of sleep, or the hundred and one other inconveniences that plague our waking hours.

⁓

Offer yourself to God through the Mass

We will indeed be fortunate if each day, or at least frequently, we are able to be present at Mass. In the Mass, we have not only the greatest incentive but the greatest opportunity to make the perfect offering of ourselves to God.

The Holy Sacrifice of the Mass is Calvary perpetuated on the altars of our churches. The same Victim of Calvary, the same Priest, our Lord Jesus Christ, offers

Himself in an unbloody manner again and again through the priesthood of His Church. Jesus offers Himself in the Mass in order that the fruits of the Redemption on Calvary may be poured forth upon the world. The offering of Jesus on the Cross was not merely a violent death, but a death that was willed by Him. He died on a Cross because He willed so to die. His offering was an act of love for man. Each day, He continues to offer Himself to the Father through the priests of the Church.

Just as the gift of Himself to the Father was not merely external but internal, so the offering of the Church, that is, the priests and the faithful, must come from the heart. If their offering is not to be merely a ritual, the priest and the faithful must, in union with the Victim of the Mass, offer themselves. Is it not the nature of every gift to express the secret thoughts and sentiments of the heart? Who is pleased to receive a gift that is given begrudgingly?

The Mass, it is true, is always a perfect act of adoration and thanksgiving, because of the High Priest Jesus Christ. But only when the Mass contains the internal offering of the priest and the faithful can it produce the desired spiritual change in them. The more generously the priest and the faithful offer themselves to God in the

Mass, the more will grace flow into their souls and draw them into close union with God. So, when we go to Mass, let our offering come from the heart.

The morning offering is not only intimately connected with the Sacrifice of the Mass, but even with the sacrament of Holy Communion. At Holy Communion, we complete the Sacrifice of the Mass by receiving within us the same Victim we offered to God. We offered God a gift; He now gives one to us. We must remember that it is a Victim we receive in Holy Communion, and, if there is to be a common union between the Victim and us, we must conform ourselves to the Victim.

Too often, Holy Communion has little effect upon us because we do not offer ourselves to Jesus in the Mass. We receive Holy Communion from force of habit, or so that we may be esteemed by our fellowman, or because it gives us consolation. If we approach the altar with such sentiments, there is no deep love of Jesus in us, no burning desire to follow in His footsteps, no generous offering of ourselves to Him. Because of this barrier, which we ourselves raise, there can be little common union between Jesus and us. But if we learn to live in the presence of God, to make the morning offering continually and sincerely, then surely it will prepare us to offer the Holy Sacrifice of the Mass, through the priest, and to receive Holy Communion in a manner that will lead us to closer and more intimate friendship with God. Let us study the Mass, think often of it, so that we may learn to offer ourselves after the manner of Jesus.

Aside from Mass and Holy Communion, let us not forget that the rest of the day, too, belongs to God. At the breakfast table — in fact, at every meal — we can renew the morning offering. It is not necessary to repeat the words of the prayer; the offering can be made mentally. We might add an aspiration, a brief prayer from the heart, if inclined, such as "My Jesus, Thy will be done!"

Offer yourself to God through the Angelus

The daily recitation of the *Angelus* prayer[48] has brought God into the everyday life of many Catholics:

The angel of the Lord declared unto Mary, and
she conceived of the Holy Spirit.
Hail Mary . . .

---

[48] The *Angelus* is traditionally prayed three times each day: in the morning, at noon, and in the evening.

"Behold the handmaid of the Lord. Be it done
unto me according to thy word."
Hail Mary . . .

And the Word was made flesh and dwelt among us.
Hail Mary . . .

Pray for us, O holy Mother of God, that we may
be made worthy of the promises of Christ.

Pour forth, we beseech Thee, O Lord, Thy grace into our
hearts, that we, to whom the Incarnation of Christ Thy Son
was made known by the message of an angel, may,
by His Passion and Cross, be brought to the glory of His
Resurrection, through the same Christ our Lord. Amen.

But the relation of the *Angelus* to the morning offering is often passed over or greatly underestimated. While
it offers us the opportunity of meditating on the mystery
of the incarnate God, it calls to our mind the great act
of oblation that Mary made to God, and it incites us to
imitate her offering. She offered her life to the total service of God when she said, "Behold the handmaid of the
Lord. Be it done unto me according to thy word."[49] This

---

[49] Luke 1:38.

surrender she continued throughout her life. It is this unselfish giving of herself that we must imitate. And nowhere do we see the complete offering of herself more convincingly expressed than when she stood beneath the Cross and offered her Son to His Father in Heaven, and offered herself in complete submission to the divine will.

When we say the *Angelus*, do we imitate the example of the Mother of God? Do we offer ourselves, or is our prayer a mere murmuring of the lips?

A practice quite common in religious life is to renew the morning offering every time a clock is heard striking the hour or the half-hour. Some may find this practice quite easy and most helpful as they go about their duties, whether they are in the home, office, store, factory, rectory, or school. In the evening, any form of relaxation or entertainment we take should be made holy by renewing the morning offering. Before retiring, we should examine our conscience to ascertain our fidelity to this practice.

⌒

All your actions should reflect your offering

The real test of the sincerity and depth of our morning offering will show itself in our reaction to daily trials and difficulties. Do we have patience with the people with whom we work? How do we accept ill health or family sickness? Are we resigned to inconveniences caused by the heat and the cold? Do we see the hand of God in these daily trials, offering them in union with the sufferings of Christ, or do we always seek our own comfort, worshiping at the shrine of self-love?

A mother must prepare her children for school each morning, must clean and dust the house, must prepare the meals, and must do the shopping. In time, this work may become almost unbearable. She may not feel well, but the work still must be done. She can do it in two ways: from dire necessity, complaining as she goes along; or she can perform it in union with Christ crucified. Is there any great toil involved in this latter way? Is it not the way Jesus would wish her to perform her tasks?

Finally, what better practice of prayer could be recommended to sick people than living in the presence of God through the morning offering? Sick people are unable at times to read or concentrate. Yet their souls would be flooded with peace if they would learn to think of God and say frequently, "Thy will be done."

Prayer will begin to flow naturally from your heart

There may be a faint suspicion that the morning offering, as we have described it, is a mere mechanical pro-
cess, a kind of forced practice that does not come from
the heart, but from a sense of duty. True, in the beginning, our prayer will not be spontaneous; it may not flow
from a heart on fire with love. But remember, it is necessary to train the mind and the will to turn to God, just as
it is necessary to train the fingers to pass quickly from key
to key on the piano.

Now, the grace of God does not do everything. It
adapts itself ordinarily to human nature, and we must
cooperate with it. We must work and have patience,
but our offering will not be a forced, unnatural practice.
It will not make us parrots. Instead, moved by the grace
of God, we will learn to want to think of God.

When we come to this state, no planned exercise
will be necessary. Our oblation will gradually flow
from the heart; it will become more dynamic, more
perfect.

It is good to remember this, because the offering of
each person is not equally pleasing to God. We may all

make the offering, but it is the love that prompts it that gives the offering its value and degree of perfection.

We should not be surprised, then, to see lukewarm Christian souls who love little, as well as very saintly souls who love much, making the morning offering. For example, we know a child who has never known the meaning of deep sorrow and privation, nor ever felt the heat of the noonday sun of temptation. This child is thrilled with the morning offering and offers his heart each day to God without fully realizing what he is doing; consequently, he offers very little to God. God has not asked the child for very much, so the child finds no difficulty in offering himself each day — just as the man with perfect health, a great deal of money, and a host of friends finds no difficulty in saying, "God is good."

That same child, when beset with adverse fortune, may not recognize the will of God, or may even go so far as to rebel against the will of God. On the other hand, a child who has a deep love of God can offer himself in a heroic manner under most difficult circumstances. Thus, Francisco, one of the three children who witnessed the apparitions of our Blessed Lady at Fatima, was able to make the most generous offering of himself at the request

of an angel who appeared to the three children. How
pleasing to Jesus must have been this offering, which he
so often repeated when the world, his friends, and even
his family ridiculed him:

> *Most Holy Trinity, Father, Son, and Holy Spirit,*
> *I adore you profoundly and offer you the most precious*
> *Body, Blood, Soul, and Divinity of Jesus Christ,*
> *present in all the tabernacles of the earth,*
> *in reparation for the outrages, sacrileges, and*
> *indifference with which He Himself is offended.*
> *And through the infinite merits of His most*
> *Sacred Heart and of the Immaculate Heart of Mary,*
> *I beg of you the conversion of poor sinners.*

During the few years he lived after the apparitions at
Fatima, Francisco learned to recognize the will of God in
the daily trials and ills of life. He welcomed them and offered them to God in reparation for sinners. The example
of Francisco is a great incentive to our own puny efforts
to give our hearts to God.

If we but turn to God to direct us along this way,
we shall surely succeed. Our offering will become more
generous, for our love will grow and even prompt us to

greater things. If we seem to be little inclined to be generous with God now, if we find the total offering of ourselves too sublime and above our power, let us not be discouraged; let us call upon God to give us the grace to make us more generous. Above all, let us not lower our standards, but, rather, keep the example of Christ crucified before our eyes. It may be His will to raise us quickly to intimate union with Him.

We can also find encouragement in the example of St. Thérèse, who in a very few years learned to make a total offering of herself, a complete surrender, to the merciful love of God. In the offering of herself, she became a victim of love and constantly experienced the loving, penetrating presence of God. Here are her own words: "Dear Mother — you who allowed me to offer myself thus to God — you know the flames of love, or rather the oceans of grace, which filled my soul when I made that Act of Oblation on June 9, 1895. Since that day, love surrounds and penetrates me; at every moment, God's Merciful Love renews and purifies me, cleansing my soul from all trace of sin."[50]

[50] *A Little White Flower*, 175.

Chapter Eight

Seek God in your soul

We have saved the good wine for the end: to think of God as He dwells within us. This way is most practical, because when we think of God within us, we are not merely imagining something that is unreal. God is really and truly within us. God is in all things — by His presence as an Observer, by His essence as Creator, and by His power as a Conserver. To His friends He is actually present in a very special way — by His grace.

This great gift of God implies more than we realize. Not only does He share His divine life with His friends, but He comes and makes His dwelling within them. The Father, the Son, and the Holy Spirit make of man a living tabernacle! How little known is this truth.

How often we look at the tabernacle in which the Sacred Host dwells, a tabernacle of steel or wood on the altar, a handmade tabernacle. We revere that tabernacle as something sacred; we decorate it, keep it spotlessly clean. The inside is lined with a white linen cloth, immaculate, because the immaculate Lamb of God rests there. But we human beings are God-made tabernacles, possessing God within us.[51]

God does not take this special dwelling in all men, but only in those who love Him: "If anyone love me, he will keep my word, and my Father will love him, and we will come to him and make our abode with him."[52]

This is the tremendous truth that St. Paul gave to his converts. Reports had reached him that the converts at Corinth were beginning to waver. Temptations, especially the allurements of the flesh, were becoming too much for some of them. To encourage them to remain steadfast in the Faith, he wrote a letter appealing to them to remember what gift they had received in Baptism: "Or do you not know that your members are the temple of the Holy Spirit, who is in you, whom you have from God, and you are not your own? For you are bought with a great price. Glorify and bear God in your body."[53]

---

[51] This indwelling is not to be confused with the presence of the Blessed Eucharist within us, whereby Christ is present with His human and divine natures as long as the uncorrupted species of bread and wine are present in us.

[52] John 14:23.

[53] 1 Cor. 6:19-20.

⌒

You can speak to God in your soul

To contemplate the indwelling of God is a way of prayer that has received the full approval of Pope Leo XIII in his encyclical on the Holy Spirit, and of Pope Pius XII in his encyclical on the Mystical Body.[54] St. Teresa long before them endorsed it for all interested in learning to love God more and more: "Remember how St. Augustine tells us about his seeking God in many places and eventually finding Him within himself. Do you suppose it is of little importance that a soul which is often distracted should come to understand this truth and to find that, in order to speak to its Eternal Father and to take its delight in Him, it has no need to go to Heaven or to speak in a loud voice? However quietly we speak, he is so near that He will hear us: we need no wings to go in search of Him, but have only to find a place where we can be alone and look upon Him present within us. Nor need we feel strange in the presence of so kind a Guest. We must talk to Him very humbly, as we should to our father, ask Him for things as we should ask a father, tell

[54] Pope Leo XIII, *Divinum illud munus*, May 9, 1897; Pope Pius XII, *Mystici Corporis Christi*, June 29, 1943.

Him our troubles, beg Him to put them right, and yet realize that we are not worthy to be called His children."

And again: "Those who are able to shut themselves up in this way within this little heaven of the soul, wherein dwells the Maker of Heaven and earth, and who have formed the habit of looking at nothing and staying in no place which will distract these outward senses, may be sure that they are walking on an excellent road, and will come without fail to drink of the water of the fountain, for they will journey a long way in a short time."[55]

A popular name among Christians in the early ages of the Church was Christopher, which means Christ-bearer. The early Christians, conscious of God dwelling in their souls, chose names that would remind them of their vocation to live with Christ.

St. Lucy,[56] one of the early Christian martyrs, learned in her youth the truth of the divine indwelling. It was the Holy Spirit within her that moved her to keep her body a pure and fit temple for Him.

---

[55] Peers, *The Complete Works of St. Teresa of Jesus*, Vol. 2, 114-115.

[56] St. Lucy (d. c. 304), martyr under the persecution by Diocletian.

In our time, the indwelling of the Blessed Trinity was the great reality in the interior life of Sr. Elizabeth of the Blessed Trinity, a Carmelite nun of Dijon, France, who died in 1906. She sought Jesus within her soul. Indeed, she believed that everyone, even laypeople, should seek Jesus within them, for she wrote to her mother, "If you read the Gospel of St. John, you will see that the Master again and again insists on this commandment, 'Abide in me and I in you.' St. John in his Epistles hopes that we may have fellowship with the Holy Trinity: this advice is so sweet and simple. It suffices — St. Paul tells us so — it suffices to believe that 'God is spirit' and it is by faith that we draw near Him.

"Give thought to the fact that your soul is 'the temple of God' — again it is St. Paul who tells you so. Every instant of the day and night, the three Divine Persons reside in you. You do not possess the Sacred Humanity, as when you receive Holy Communion, but the Divinity. The Divinity whom the blessed adore in Heaven is in your soul. Once you are aware of this, it is a most delightful intimacy; you are never alone again. If you prefer to think that the good God is near you rather than in you, follow your preference, provided that you live with Him. . . .

Reflect that you are with Him, and act as you do with someone you love. It is so simple: there is no need of beautiful thoughts; all that is necessary is simply an outpouring of the heart."[57]

Awareness of God's indwelling deepens your love

After long and deep consideration of the divine indwelling, we begin to realize that Christianity is something we *live*, that it is a life given by Christ that grows, and this growth is one of union with God, who dwells as a lover within the heart of man. Human love grows; two hearts begin to beat as one, two wills to act as one. Such, also, is the love of man and God. Thinking of God within us, we begin to see things the way He sees them. We begin to will what God wills.

Once conscious of bearing God, we begin to talk to Him. We call out to Him, even in the heat of great work. We can do this because just a few words — even a sigh — suffice to convey our thoughts and desires to the

---

[57] M. M. Philipon, O.P., *La Doctrine Spirituelle de Souer Elizabeth de la Trinité* (Montreal: Granger Frères, n.d.), 112. The English edition is *The Spiritual Doctrine of Sister Elizabeth of the Trinity* (Westminster, Maryland: Newman Press, 1951), 70-71. — ED.

indwelling God. When we grow more perfect in this, when our soul is in the continual presence of God, we send forth aspirations of love — *breathings forth*, in the full sense of the word.

We often hear and read about the "Christian way of life." For some people, this is a vague and intangible expression. In reality, it means precisely what we have just described — namely, a life of common interest with God; a life in which this love of God dominates all our thoughts, words, and actions. The greater the love, the more Christian the life. Whatever we eat, drink, say, write, or do, it should come from our soul living in conscious union and silent conversation with God. It is this union with God that colors our whole life and makes it Christian.

When enough of us are conscious of this union and guided by it in our thoughts and actions, there will be a change in our country's philosophy. When men and women, conscious of their calling, actually live in union of love with God in their daily lives, our politics, our literature, and our entertainment will become really Christian.

The world will become Christian when men become Christian.

To think of the indwelling of God takes but a moment. The imagination may or may not be called into play. But we should repeat this act continually. It does cost some effort, it does presuppose dogged perseverance, but it does not lead to nervous strain or headaches.

It is a simple act, especially for beginners: "My God within me, I love Thee." We can think of God within us when we are alone. We can think of Him in a crowded subway, as we walk along a busy street, or as we sit in a classroom or run a lathe in a machine shop. We can think of Him as we stand over a stove or as we write a letter. We can think of Him as we bathe the wounds of the sick.

This continual practice does not mean that we reflect on God every moment of the day and night. Rather, it means that we are in a state of union with God, and from time to time we become conscious of this and break forth easily into an act of prayer.

But will this life make us introverts, self-centered? No, it will make us God-centered and neighbor-conscious. When we see our neighbor suffering, then, like Christ, we will want to help him. We will want to be like Him who gave His life that others might have life, and have it more abundantly.[58] We will see God dwelling in the soul of our neighbor.

What a great effect the practice of the divine indwelling could have on the morals of society! Today, the world has lost the virtue of purity. We lack it in our cities as much as the Corinthians did in the days of St. Paul. But it could be restored to society if we were to look upon human beings as the living tabernacles of God, too sacred to be polluted. What better way could we restore the doctrine of the dignity of man, now vanishing among nations, than by seeing God dwelling within the souls of men, lifting all men up to be His sacred tabernacles?

Behold the dignity of man!

[58] Cf. John 10:10.

Part Three

How to begin to
walk with God daily

Chapter Nine

Raise your heart to God in aspirations

God in our thoughts, God in our hearts, God on our lips,
loving awareness of God, affective presence of God —
this will be our happy state once we have put into practice the different ways of living in God's presence.

Two acts, *thinking* of God and *loving* God, make up the
exercise of the presence of God. Thinking of God leads
to loving Him. These two acts should not be divorced,
any more than a flower should be torn from its stem. We
have already considered five ways that help us to think of
God and to acquire recollection. Let us now consider the
acts of the will by which we can fan this recollection into
flaming love for God. This is the goal upon which the
five ways converge, and this direction of our will, from a
practical standpoint, is more important than the acts of
the intellect by which we think of God. Prayer consists
not so much in merely thinking of God as in loving Him.

Dogged perseverance in the art of thinking of God
will draw our hearts into closer union with our divine

Friend, who, in turn, will gently urge us to desire to do
His will, to long for greater intimacy with Him, and to
speak to Him the language of love. When we have arrived
at this stage, we find that acts of love and praise come
more easily to us. We find ourselves turning to God
within us, addressing Him with short, fervent acts of
hope, love, and praise — acts that flow naturally and
easily, and at times with the rhythmic regularity of our
breathing. When these acts are frequent and regular, they
are a sign that we have fallen deeply in love with God
and now enjoy true intimate friendship with Him. These
hidden desires, these expressions of love, we call aspirations, or the prayer of aspirations.

Aspirations express your love for God

What, precisely, is an aspiration, or the prayer of aspirations? An aspiration, like prayer in general, is an elevation of the mind to God. But it is an elevation that is
impelled by love, composed of only a few words, and
directed like a dart to God, that He may know the holy
affections and desires of the soul. Like arrows that shoot
directly toward their target, these prayers leap, as it were,
from the soul directly to God.

Strictly speaking, not all short prayers are aspirations, although we often call them such, because aspirations are the effect of actual charity, expressions of love that burns in the soul. We know that some short prayers are able to be motivated by faith and hope without charity. For example, a person in mortal sin might call out to God to be relieved from terrible physical pain. Such a prayer, motivated by faith and hope in the power of God, may appear to be an aspiration, but, in the sense that we use the word, it is not such.

Aspirations, in their full sense, must be born of love, of actual charity which moves the soul to cry out to God.

Aspirations, therefore, are expressions of love, sighs of the hidden desires of the soul. They are not long, drawn-out prayers, but consist in a very few words, as for example, "My God, I love Thee." When these desires of love are prolonged and a loving conversation ensues between the soul and God, this prayer is no longer called the prayer of aspirations, but a colloquy.

Not all lovers love with the same ardor, and since aspirations have their foundation in love, it follows that the state of their perfection will vary with the degree of love that motivates them. We find people who practice aspirations rarely, and others, overwhelmed with love, who, as it were, seem to cling to God, breathing forth the desires of the soul almost constantly and without any previous consideration of the intellect. Love runs away from and oversteps the ordinary processes of thinking. God comes into the mind of such people, and in a moment they think of Him and desire to be always united to Him. Even though it seems that there is no clear concept of God in the mind, the will seems to be directly moved by Him and the whole soul drawn into union with Him. This often happens to very holy people.

☞

Aspirations can increase your love for God

We, however, must not wait to be drawn by God in this manner. Such attraction is a gift that God gives to whom He wills and when He wills. Let us correspond with the ordinary grace God gives us and enkindle by aspirations the fire of love in our soul. Let our love become more actual, more ardent, and more constant, so that aspirations become our habitual manner of prayer. It seems that St. Thérèse prayed in this manner, for she writes, "For me prayer is an uplifting of the heart, a glance toward Heaven, a cry of gratitude and of love in times of sorrow as well as joy."[59]

This *going out* toward God, this loving awareness, is what really makes for intimate friendship. God, delighted with our love, responds with His own shafts of love, His divine graces, and, in a short time, the soul finds itself deeply in love with Him, conversing with Him in a most friendly manner.

It would be a tragic mistake to identify the heart afire in the prayer of aspirations with joyous emotions and consolation. The aspirations, the desires, the sighs come from the soul and not from the senses. Even a soul steeped in sorrow may have them, for the prayer of aspirations is not an ecstasy of love that you can feel. It is true love that blooms in a desert of sorrow as well as in a paradise of joy. The feeling of joy may come or go, but the soul remains rooted in God, making known its desires to Him.

It is obvious by now that when aspirations flow with regularity and have become habitual, the soul is well advanced in prayer and has accustomed itself to live in the presence of God. Indeed, many spiritual writers consider

[59] A *Little White Flower*, 219.

the prayer of aspirations as the prayer of more perfect souls, as the fruit of fidelity to meditation. And rightly so.

⤢

Let your aspirations arise out of love

But what of the beginner in the spiritual life? Is there no place for the prayer of aspirations in his life? Must he wait until he acquires the state of recollection? No. He, too, can use aspirations with great profit. His aspirations will not be the effect of deep love, but, rather, an attempt to excite more love. In such souls, aspirations can be used as a way to place the soul in the affective presence of God. How valuable aspirations can be to all of us, no matter how shallow our love, can be seen from the advice of St. Francis de Sales to Philothea: "This habit of spiritual retirement and the prayer of aspirations is the keystone of devotion, and can supply the defects of all your other prayers; but nothing else can supply its place. Without it, you cannot follow the contemplative life well, nor the active life without danger. Without it, repose is but idleness, labor but trouble: therefore, I beseech you, cleave steadily to it, and never forsake it."[60]

[60] St. Francis de Sales (1567-1622; Bishop of Geneva), *Introduction to the Devout Life*, Part 2, ch. 13.

In view of this advice, it seems most advisable to explain in some detail how beginners should employ aspirations. In the first place, let us dispel what might be a common error — namely, that an increase in the daily output of aspirations is progress. On the contrary, real progress in aspirations is measured by our growth in the love of God. One aspiration from the heart is worth more in the art of love than one hundred aspirations that tumble mechanically from the lips.

Should we, then, discourage people who recite a number of memorized aspirations each day? Certainly not. We should encourage them, but let them realize that this is just the beginning. God demands more! He wants the aspirations to come from the depths of our hearts. He is more interested in the intensity than in the number. He wants us to pray naturally, simply, as a child speaks to his father. In this we have the example of the Little Flower, who said, "I say just what I want to say to God, quite simply, and He never fails to understand."[61]

If we are just beginning the practice of the presence of God, our aspirations will probably be few and not very

---

[61] *A Little White Flower*, 219.

natural. We must remember that the constant effort to use all occasions, all persons and things, to remind us of God will eventually bring our souls to fervent aspirations. And in the meantime, if no aspirations come naturally to us, we can use the ready-made aspirations of the saints or of Sacred Scripture. This use of ready-made aspirations, rather than being a forced practice, might even be called, as we have said before, another way to live in God's presence, because the aspirations help keep our minds recollected, centered on God. It is well worthwhile to memorize those aspirations that appeal to us, provided that we do not content ourselves with mere mechanical recitation of them.

It may happen that one particular aspiration suggests itself and is especially beneficial in keeping the mind and heart on God. In such a case, it would be foolish to look for variety. Remember the oft-told story of St. Francis of Assisi,[62] who passed a whole night repeating slowly to himself this one prayer: "My Lord and my God!" Intensity of love, not variety of prayers, counts in our life with God.

[62] St. Francis of Assisi (c. 1182-1226), founder of the Franciscan Order.

It is said that an Irish chaplain offered God a hundred thousand aspirations daily during World War I. How he counted them we do not know. Yet, it would be difficult to prove that such intensive prayer is impossible. One thing is certain: we need not count our aspirations or the number of times we think of God. Perhaps faulty education in this fundamental point may be responsible for our almost total neglect of aspirations. A child, for instance, who for the entire Advent season made a thousand or more hasty aspirations a day, in hot competition with other members of his class for the honor of bringing the most "straws" for the infant Jesus to lie upon, is apt in later life to regard the practice of aspirations as senseless and repellent. Here, the original idea, to show and develop love for Christ, has often been perverted into the American system of mass-production, with the result that the child is too busy for love. We please God by loving Him and opening our souls to the Holy Spirit for enlightenment and inspiration.

Those advanced in prayer need no booklet of aspirations. Their meditations and state of recollection will give them many holy thoughts to inflame their hearts. And a heart inflamed breaks forth naturally in loving aspirations. The exercise of the presence of God, with the accent on aspirations, should be the natural fruit of fidelity to daily meditation. Hence, priests and religious who are obliged to meditate daily should use their meditations as an aid to fervent aspirations, rather than neglect it under the pretext that they practice the presence of God and use aspirations frequently each day. Yet, when they are unable to make their daily meditation, for example, when sick or traveling, the use of frequent aspirations will be a most fitting substitute.

☞

The prayer of aspirations is for all times and places

Occasionally, we meet people who like to pray in quiet places or in church and, because they abhor a public manifestation of piety, look askance at the prayer of aspirations, which is recommended for all times and places. Such people should be reminded that the prayer of aspirations does not always call for vocal prayer or for the moving of the lips. Since the aspirations are really the desires and affections of the heart, they need not be externally manifested.

There are other people who like to give God just so much of their time and no more, lest He interfere with

their work. Aside from the obvious rejoinder that God
has given them the day only so that they may save their
souls, we can tell these people that there need be no con-
flict between their work and prayer. It is impossible to be
deeply occupied with both work and prayer at the same
time. But at least we can always turn our minds to God
and away from useless or even sinful thoughts, whenever
there is a moment free from other mental work. And
we can train ourselves to be so habitually inclined to
God that, even when engaged in strenuous tasks, we
can raise our hearts to Him from time to time in the
prayer of aspirations.

St. Bernardine of Siena[63] had special aspirations
for each day of the week. For example, on Sunday: "O
Good Jesus, make me love Thee ardently!" Monday:
"Jesus, sweet Love, make me feel with what unbounded
love You have loved us, and still love us!" Tuesday: "Most
loving Jesus, I would love Thee, but, without Thee, I
cannot."

We can imitate this practice of St. Bernardine, chang-
ing the aspirations if we find such bursts of ardent love

[63] St. Bernardine of Siena (1380-1444), Franciscan
reformer.

out of harmony with our own imperfect state of soul. Certainly, none of us who are really sorry for our sins should find it difficult to substitute the following aspirations: "Jesus, have mercy on us." "Jesus, forgive my sins." "Help me never to sin again." "Jesus, teach me to love Thee." These are just suggestions. Let each one, guided by the Holy Spirit, choose his own.

Those who recite the Divine Office and read the Scriptures have abundant material at their disposal. During Advent, it would be easy and helpful to prepare for the feast of Christmas by repeating frequently each day the following verses from the Advent Office:

> Drop down dew, ye heavens above,
> and let the clouds rain down the Just One!
>
> Let the earth open and bud forth a Savior!
>
> Send now, we beg Thee, O Lord,
> send Him whom Thou art to send!
>
> Come, O Lord, and visit us in Thy peace.

Throughout the year, and especially during Lent, verses from the Divine Office can supply our daily aspirations. How simple it would be to repeat often the verses of the *Miserere*.[64] And when we are inclined to praise God, we can choose no better aspiration than "Glory be to the Father, and to the Son, and to the Holy Spirit, as it was in the beginning, is now, and ever shall be, world without end. Amen."

The prayer of aspirations, to repeat, admits of many degrees. If we are beginning the practice of the presence of God, we can use aspirations to keep our minds on Him. If we are already recollected, already living with God, we will find our souls moved to break forth in fervent bursts of love, for this is the prayer of aspirations in its full growth. In this state, we should give free reign to these holy desires, recognizing them as the reward for living in God's presence. They are a sign that we are deeply in love with God, that we are already engaged in a loving conversation with Him.

The more frequent and fervent these desires and longings become, the more brightly will love burn in our souls. And for this God created us.

[64] Ps. 50 (RSV = Ps. 51).

Chapter Ten

Welcome God into your life

There are moments in life when we feel alone and help-less, even though God is present. There are times when God seems to forget us, just as a child, tired of his toys, throws them into a corner and forgets them. But God will never leave us, although we may desert Him. He may not make His presence felt; He may not even give joy. But He is always with us. His love will never grow cold. He does not wish us to walk alone.

God wants to be with us. He is always conscious of us, more conscious of us than we are of ourselves. He wants us to be aware of His abiding presence as we tread the beaten ways. For this reason, He descended from the stars and began to walk with us. He became a child so that we might be drawn to know and to love Him more. He became the divine Teacher so that we might learn from Him, the Model and Light of our life. He died upon a Cross, and rose again from the dead to bring divine life into our souls. And now, although He has ascended into

Heaven, He still abides with us in the Holy Eucharist, our food and our joy. He has even sent His Holy Spirit to whisper to us all truth and gently to move our wills to conform with His. God is always with us, and in many ways.

Too many people, unmindful of the merciful love of God, have given Him too little time in their lives. They look intently at themselves; they hardly ever look at God. In themselves they have not found the answer to their problems. They have found fear, loneliness, sin, and despair. Let them take courage and turn to God. He is not far away. He is the life of their souls. A tree will not grow if left alone; unless it has sun and rain, it withers and dies. If we take God out of our lives and try to live without Him, the life of our souls will surely wither and die. And when a whole nation, or at least its influential leaders, lives without God, the death knell for the nation has already begun to toll.

If we wish to live a full life, really to attain the purpose of our creation, God must be given His rightful place in our lives. We must continually look at Him, listen to Him, talk with Him, and walk with Him.

Let us not walk alone.

We have proposed different ways to live in the presence of God. One way does not exclude the others. All are valuable insofar as they lead us to divine friendship. If we find them helpful, let us persevere in their use. If they leave us cold and far from God, let us choose other means.

But whether these ways are helpful or not, let us never lose the desire to be the intimate friends of God. Without this desire, we cannot expect to know God well or love Him deeply. Should we lack this desire, let us take courage and pray earnestly for it, because the one important thing is to know God intimately and to love Him with all the love of our hearts. Our hearts were made for love and they will not rest in peace until they rest in God. For God is love.

Part Four

Prayers to help you
walk with God daily

⇌

⇌ The Angelus ⇋

The angel of the Lord declared unto Mary,
and she conceived of the Holy Spirit.
Hail Mary . . .

"Behold the handmaid of the Lord.
Be it done unto me according to thy word."
Hail Mary . . .

And the Word was made flesh
and dwelt among us.
Hail Mary . . .

Pray for us, O holy Mother of God, that we may
be made worthy of the promises of Christ.

Pour forth, we beseech Thee, O Lord, Thy grace into
our hearts, that we, to whom the Incarnation of Christ
Thy Son was made known by the message of an angel, may,
by His Passion and Cross, be brought to the glory of His
Resurrection, through the same Christ our Lord. Amen.

ᴥ Morning Offering ᴥ

O Jesus, through the Immaculate Heart of Mary,
I offer Thee my prayers, works, and sufferings of this day
in union with the Holy Sacrifice of the Mass throughout
the world, in reparation for my sins, and for the
intentions recommended by the Holy Father.

ᴥ Morning Offering ᴥ
(short form)

Jesus, through the Immaculate Heart of Mary,
I offer Thee this day all my thoughts, words,
actions, joys, and sufferings.

ᴥ Prayer of Francisco of Fatima ᴥ

Most Holy Trinity, Father, Son, and Holy Spirit,
I adore you profoundly and offer you the most
precious Body, Blood, Soul, and Divinity of Jesus Christ,
present in all the tabernacles of the earth, in reparation
for the outrages, sacrileges, and indifference with which He
Himself is offended. And through the infinite merits of His
Most Sacred Heart and of the Immaculate Heart of Mary,
I beg of you the conversion of poor sinners.

Biographical Note

Kilian J. Healy, O. Carm.

Born in Worcester, Massachusetts, in 1912, Kilian J. Healy was ordained a Carmelite priest in Rome in 1937. In addition to serving as the Prior General of his order, Fr. Healy was a voting member of the Second Vatican Council, and he taught theology and philosophy in the United States and in Rome. He currently serves at the Carmelite Gift Shop and Catholic Information Center in Peabody, Massachusetts.

Drawing on the rich spirituality of the Carmelite Order, especially on the wisdom of St. Teresa of Avila and St. Thérèse of Lisieux, Fr. Healy calls all Christians to answer God's call to friendship with Him and offers a simple, practical path to experiencing the joy of living always in the presence of God.

Sophia Institute Press®

An Invitation

Reader, the book that you hold in your hands was published by Sophia Institute Press. Sophia Institute seeks to nurture the spiritual, moral, and cultural life of souls and to spread the Gospel of Christ in conformity with the authentic teachings of the Roman Catholic Church.

Our press fulfills this mission by offering translations, reprints, and new publications that afford readers a rich source of the enduring wisdom of mankind.

We also operate two popular online Catholic resources: CrisisMagazine.com and CatholicExchange.com.

Crisis Magazine provides insightful cultural analysis that arms readers with the arguments necessary for navigating the ideological and theological minefields of the day. *Catholic Exchange* provides world news from a Catholic perspective as well as daily devotionals and articles that will help you to grow in holiness and live a life consistent with the teachings of the Church.

Sophia Institute Press also serves as the publisher for the Thomas More College of Liberal Arts and Holy Spirit College. Both colleges provide university-level education under the guiding light of Catholic teaching. If you know a young person seeking a college that takes seriously the adventure of learning and the quest for truth, please bring these institutions to his attention.

www.SophiaInstitute.com
www.CatholicExchange.com
www.CrisisMagazine.com